© 2013
JUSTIN GLANVILLE, JULIA KUO, LEE ZELENAK
WWW.THE-BEAGLE.COM

All rights reserved. No part of this book may be reproduced in any form without written permission of the copyright owner.

First published in the United States
by Beagle Publishing

ISBN: 978-0-615-91325-4

Written by: Justin Glanville
Illustrated by: Julia Kuo
Art Direction & Design: Lee Zelenak, Kiddo Design

CONTENTS

1:	Introduction	5
2:	About This Book	9
3:	How We Hide	13
4:	How to Stop Hiding in Your Process	19
5:	How to Stop Hiding in Your Language	37
6:	In Closing	53
7:	Further Reading	56

INTRODUCTION

This book is designed to teach you how to write without hiding. What exactly does "writing without hiding" mean? It means that you're being as clear and honest as possible in your writing — both in your writing process and the language you use. You are choosing to *be* yourself rather than *obscure* yourself.

You might not think of yourself as a writer who hides. "I do struggle with writing," you may think. "Sometimes — or often — I don't enjoy writing. On bad days, I think I'm pretty much the worst writer ever to disgrace the planet. But I don't think I hide."

Fair enough. But this book challenges you to think of those difficulties in a different way. What if they resulted not from a lack of talent or skill, but from an entirely human tendency to hide? And what if you could learn not to hide?

If you're like most people, you've done one or more of the following:

- Rushed through a first draft and presented it as final because you don't have the time or patience to revise
- Given up on a project because you're "not good enough"
- Chosen a subject matter or genre of writing that you think other people will enjoy, even though you find it deadly dull
- Written super-long sentences or used fancy words because you think they will impress readers

The common thread? These are all behaviors that obscure both yourself and your message. They are ways of hiding. As a result, they keep you from connecting with other people. And that's no good, because connection and communication are the very purpose of writing — some might even say of life.

WRITING IN THE NEW ECONOMY

Connecting with other people is important nowadays. It always has been — human beings are a social species. But today's economy increasingly rewards those who know how to make deep connections with others.

Think about the way marketing works today. The old interruption-based way of selling products through advertising is extinct. People have nearly unlimited choices about how and what they consume. Don't like a TV show or a website or news article? Switch to one of the billions of others — instantaneously. Assaulted by an ad you don't want to see? Look elsewhere.

To succeed in this New Economy — what Seth Godin and others call the Connection Economy — is to cut through the clutter and connect with people who want what you're offering. And to want it, they have to understand it. That's why learning to write without hiding has never been more important.

You say you're not writing for the money? You just want to find an audience or please a boss or teacher? Same thing: All about connection, and connection comes from clarity and honesty.

In the United States and other post-industrial countries, more and more work requires us to write clearly and well.

Whether you end up employed by a company or working for yourself, consider how many jobs now depend on the generation of ideas. In human resources, in technology, in mental health professions, in traditionally "creative" fields like arts and design, we're all looking for ways to say things that will connect with other people. Things that will matter.

And yes, we'll express a lot of those ideas through speech — or sometimes visual art or HTML or some other medium. But writing remains the most portable and consumable form of expression. Email, websites, reports, books, papers, Facebook, Twitter: Their foundation is the written word.

Here's Jason Fried, founder of 37Signals, a web application development company:

> "If you are trying to decide among a few people to fill a position, hire the best writer. It doesn't matter if the person is a marketer, salesperson, designer, programmer, or whatever; their writing skills will pay off."

He goes on to say that "clear writing is a sign of clear thinking," and that the rise of social media and text messaging demonstrates that "writing is today's currency for good ideas."

You may be reading this book because you want to write better reports for work. You may want better grades on your school papers. You may want more readers for your blog. You may be trying to find your voice as a fiction writer or essayist.

They're all great reasons. And they all point you down the same path: Stop hiding.

ABOUT THIS BOOK

Before I go on preaching, let me make a confession: I'm an expert writing hider. Over the years, I've often been paralyzed by fears that I'm a big old impostor with no talent (p. 21). I've spent months or years planning projects without getting started writing them (p. 24). I've dismissed my ideas as boring (p. 22). I've used the smoke and mirrors of fancy language to try to impress others (p. 51).

In short, I've pretty much done everything I warn about in this book — even though for years I've made my living at least in part from writing. That takes some doing, folks.

I remember one of my first wake-up calls about hiding. It happened in college, where I majored in Classics — the study of ancient Greek and Roman culture. One day, toward the end of my senior year, I was sitting in my advisor's office, waiting for his feedback on my thesis paper.

He leaned over his desk and gave me a little smile. He said something I still remember, verbatim, to this day: "The gorgon of your gorgiastic prose has turned me to stone." You probably gather that's not a compliment. But since it's practically in a foreign language, allow me to unpack it for you a bit.

In Greek mythology, the gorgons were three really ugly sisters. You've heard of Medusa? She was one of them. Medusa and her sibs had hair made out of poisonous snakes and wore big, frightening grins. They ran around turning anyone who looked at them to stone. My paper concerned how Greek artists depicted these ladies on vases and wall paintings.

"Gorgiastic" rhetoric, meanwhile, refers to the Greek philosopher Gorgias. His much more famous contemporary, Socrates, liked to make fun of Gorgias' long, empty sentences. Socrates invented the term "Gorgiastic" to refer to language stuffed full of empty calories: Poorly argued points adorned with useless adjectives, adverbs and dependent clauses.

The translation of my advisor's feedback? Your writing has too much style, too little substance.

I was pretty mad at my advisor back then. I thought he was mean. I spent a few days — OK, more than a week — sulking about what he'd said. But then I got down to work and did what I needed to do: More research. More thinking about what I was trying to say. Clearer language, less wordiness.

And my paper got better. Not perfect, but better.

The "gorgon" statement has guided my writing ever since — in my jobs as a reporter and urban planner, and also in my creative writing and journaling. It also gave this book its monster theme, the idea that hiding techniques are monsters that we can subdue through awareness.

THE GORGON OF YOUR GORGIASTIC PROSE HAS TURNED ME TO STONE.

You know that old adage, teach what you want to learn? That's the philosophy behind this book. As much as I hope it's a guide for others, it's also a challenge to myself to stay honest in my own writing. It's like what Austin Kleon says in his book *Steal Like an Artist*: The advice he gives is what his adult self would tell his younger self. Even his one-day-younger self.

So now that we're all in this together, let's get started.

HOW W

E HIDE

HOW WE HIDE

Different people hide for different reasons. Some may lack confidence. Others haven't prepared enough to know what they want to say. Still others may be telling themselves that they don't care about writing, hiding behind the persona of the "non-writer" even though that's debilitating in today's economy.

These aren't things anyone should feel bad about. They could stem from any number of common external or internal factors. You got discouraging feedback from your third-grade teacher, for example. Or maybe it's in your nature to please others first. And heck, just about everyone in today's society feels the need to rush. To produce, produce, produce even if they haven't had time to prepare.

This book provides some tools that will help you see past all that stuff. What you'll find are not so much rigid instructions as ways to overcome the hiding mentality. Best news of all? No exercises, and no homework! For me, change happens subtly and often slowly. So think of the advice in this book as seeds planted in your mind. Let them take root over time.

THE TWO WAYS OF HIDING

There are two main ways of hiding in writing: In the *process* and in the *language*.

Hiding in the process involves using inefficient or self-defeating writing techniques. Hiding in the language are ways of obscuring meaning by using passive voice, fancy vocabulary, cliches and other crutches.

So how do you know you're hiding? Here are some signs:

HIDING IN THE PROCESS

- *You tell yourself you can't write, that you either don't care or don't have "talent."*
- *You choose (or accept from others) topics you find dull because you think they will interest someone else.*
- *You start with answers instead of questions.*
- *You begin writing before you have enough to say. (Common when we have deadlines or are impatient.)*
- *Or the opposite: You get stuck in an endless research-and-preparation loop. (Common when we don't have deadlines.)*

- *You antagonize instead of use your deadlines, waiting until the last minute to start work.*
- *You tweak sentences you've already written instead of moving ahead.*
- *You finish an first draft, but then refuse to revise it.*

HIDING IN THE LANGUAGE

- *You give in to the temptations of lazy writing: passive voice construction, the verb "to be," clichés, and lots of mentions of a mysterious creature called "It."*
- *You rely on verbal costume jewelry: long sentences, semicolons, adverbs and fancy language.*

Do you see yourself in any or all of the above points? If so, welcome. Welcome to the I Like to Hide Club. It's a very human club. Just about everyone in the world either is a member or has been one — myself included.

Luckily, there are some simple practices to help you stop hiding. Let's get right to the cheat sheet, and we'll discuss them in detail later.

HOW TO STOP HIDING: THE WRITING PROCESS

- *Embrace the fact that you can learn to write, and that in today's world writing is how you are most likely to be heard.*
- *Trust yourself and your instincts, and choose topics that interest you.*
- *Start with questions instead of answers.*
- *Do enough but not too much preparation and research, including making a road map of your paper (don't worry, I didn't say "outline"!).*
- *Write forward instead of backward.*
- *Don't be afraid of your first draft. Instead, take it on a date.*
- *Use, don't antagonize, your deadline.*

HOW TO STOP HIDING: LANGUAGE

- *Steer clear of language hobgoblins by using active voice construction, throwing away the "to be" crutch, being aware of your use of cliches and your use of "it."*

- *Choose substance over style.*

- *Liberate your sentences to be short and to the point.*

HOW TO STOP HIDING IN YOUR PROCESS

HOW TO STOP HIDING IN YOUR PROCESS

The biggest obstacles that most writers face have nothing to do with writing per se — that is, the use of language, the typing of words into a computer. Instead, they have to do with the way we choose to write, our methods of working.

There are dozens of books out there that give you step-by-step instructions for developing a better or more efficient writing process. They can be quite helpful, especially if you treat them as experiments and remember that no single book or guru has The Answer. Your process will be like your fingerprints: Different from anyone else's.

This book aims for something different. It will teach you new ways of thinking that will soothe the common anxieties people feel about writing. These new ways of thinking will help you 1) get started writing and then 2) keep going.

Important note: Your impulse to hide in your writing at any given time corresponds to the broader picture of your life. If you're not feeling so great about Life as Yourself, it's going to be hard to write freely, even with the ideas in this book. Things like therapy, exercise, socializing with friends and restorative hobbies provide a vital groundwork for creating. Those steps are outside the scope of this book but they will support your work here.

REALIZE THAT YOU — YES, YOU — CAN WRITE.

We all love the romantic idea of "talent" — this universe/God-given ability to do something better than other people can.

Problem is, talent matters barely a fig when it comes to producing clear, compelling writing.

Sure, some people might be born with a natural predilection for language. But for one thing, that doesn't mean other people can't develop the same or similar skill. Most of us can speak, can't we? That's a skill we develop over months or years of practice. Written language is the same: something we hone over years of practice.

And anyway, writing isn't primarily about language. That sounds odd, but it's true. Writing, first and foremost, is a means to express ourselves and our ideas. It's about being honest. It's not about showing off how beautiful your sentences are or how fancy your vocabulary.

The notion of talent, that some people have it and some don't, probably silences more writers than any other single factor.

And not just for people who've been told they don't have much talent. Being told you *do* have talent may be even more crippling, because you end up thinking you have a responsibility to produce beautiful prose all the time, every time. What a burden, and what a killer of creativity!

Even if there were such a thing as talent, producing clear writing is hard work. As author E.L. Konigsberg says: "The difference between being a writer and being a person of talent is the discipline it takes to apply the seat of your pants to the seat of your chair and finish."

So stop labeling yourself as either talented or untalented. Your job is just to write in a way that's clear and honest.

TRUST YOURSELF AND YOUR INSTINCTS

The key to any good writing is to find a concept that genuinely interests you. If you're bored by your own concept, the writing will be torture for you. And if you hate the writing, your reader is nearly guaranteed to hate the reading.

Sometimes a teacher or boss assigns the concept, and maybe you think it's a drag. First of all, if this happens often, you might ask yourself whether you're in the right field. Seriously. It's a tough question, but wouldn't you rather ask it now than at your retirement party? More often than not, though, you have some freedom about what to explore.

The idea of honoring your interests may sound self-evident. But the boss-pleasing, professor-pleasing, audience-pleasing impulse can be sneaky. I'm always surprised how many students approach me fretting about what they "should" write. I understand why: They want to do well, to be liked. That's what our culture teaches.

Here's the thing: The best way to impress your readers is not to pick The Perfect Topic, but to engage them on what you do pick. And the best way to engage is to be engaged yourself.

You can't fake interest. No matter how much you gussy up your writing (see p. 37), or wave your arms in the air and ACT REALLY EXCITED! when you're talking, people will know if you're faking. Think about the last time you heard someone speak about something they found uninteresting. It's bad enough when they act bored, right? But it's just as transparent — and even annoying — when they're pretending they're not.

Sometimes, a topic will interest you initially but you realize as you go that you aren't feeling it. Change course. Yes, you will have lost some time up front, but attaching to something that isn't working leads to one, and only one, outcome: Misery. For the writer and the reader.

Before you start a writing project, do a solo brainstorming session. Write down every subject or idea you think might be interesting. The ideas don't need to be highly specific, because you'll be honing them as you go (see p. 24). If the project has limits because of a work or school assignment, be aware of those limits, but don't be afraid to push at their boundaries. Then review your list. Which topic excites you the most? If more than one does, is there a way you can combine those into one concept?

Another way to think about this is to promise yourself never to judge or censor your own ideas. Try them first. Try your first instinct, not your second or your third. By the time you get to second and third instincts, you're probably listening to someone else's voice anyway. Try what you want, and only if it doesn't work out do you move on.

START WITH QUESTIONS INSTEAD OF ANSWERS

Novelist Caroline Leavitt starts every new writing project with a question. The question is what excites her. It's what drives her to stick with her project for the hundreds of pages and multiple drafts and the many hours she'll need to finish. How far will a mother go to protect her child? What happens to two friends driven apart by childhood tragedy?

The same is true in nonfiction writing, even if you're writing a report or paper that's only five pages instead of 300: Questions, not answers, compel. They compel writers and they compel readers, too.

A central question can be the fuel that keeps you interested in your writing. It can also provide a North Star for when you feel you've gone off the tracks, and re-energize you when you're feeling low.

And yet so often we try to start with answers. We recite what we think we already know, or worse, what we've been told. Let's say you're writing a thesis paper. You may come up with one of the following thesis statements to get started:

- Psychotherapy combined with medication leads to the longest-lasting improvements for most patients suffering from depression.
- Atlantic Ocean fisheries have declined precipitously in the last 20 years.

They're both answers rather than questions, and they both put you in a crate. Starting with an answer limits you to a preordained conclusion. This denies the very nature of writing and any other truly creative act, which is exploration. Compelling writing explores; flat writing imposes.

There's more energy in a question. Something like these:

- For what kind of depression patient does a combination of therapies work best? Do those patients exhibit any shared characteristics?
- In what ways have Atlantic Ocean fisheries declined in the last 20 years? What are the most promising methods for restoring them?

Yes, in a paper for school or work, you may eventually have to come up with a thesis statement. But don't do it right away. Starting with a question, and continuing to engage it throughout the writing, will force you to seek out real answers, not cling to the ones you already have. That may scare you, but it's also what will keep you and your reader awake.

What about when you're given a question, as in a grant report questionnaire or the dreaded college entrance essay? In one way this isn't ideal, because maybe the question doesn't thrill you. But in another way it's great, because right up front you're prompted to explore rather than report. In any case, the technique is the same: Engage the question rather than leaping to answers.

THE GOLDILOCKS METHOD OF PREPARATION: ENOUGH BUT NOT TOO MUCH!

When you have deadlines, the tendency is to rush the preparation. To Google around for a few hours, find a few sources. Skip the library. Skip outlining. Jump right into writing.

The opposite can happen when you don't have a deadline, when you're working on your own schedule. You Google endlessly. Outline forever. Haunt libraries and become fascinated by the interlibrary loan system, through which you can check out this amazing-sounding graduate dissertation that's only available at the community college library in Terre Haute, Indiana!

In both cases, of course, fear drives the (lack of) action. Lack of preparation and too much preparation are both strategies to avoid writing something that will be heard. They are two different responses to the insecure voice deep within: "I'm not good enough to be heard," which sometimes disguises itself as "I don't care about being heard." In the first case, you run from the voice. You avoid it by tossing off a paper that's way below your capabilities. In the second, you feed it more and more ammunition. ("Wow, check out all this stuff I don't know. Check out how many other people have already done a really good job writing about this! Who do I think I am?")

What's the way through? Make like Goldilocks: Look for juuuust right. Look for enough.

How do you know when you've prepared enough? Bad news: That's a question you'll have to ask yourself each time you work on a new project. There's no hard and fast rule. It's just like eating. You want to end up feeling full, not hungry or overstuffed.

And of course, different types of writing call for different types of preparation. Personal essays, memoir and realistic fiction may not require much research at all. Marketing reports, speculative fiction, nonfiction books and term papers may require a ton.

Here are a few ideas for doing effective research:

SCHEDULING YOUR RESEARCH

Whether you tend to underprepare or overprepare, a schedule can help. Give yourself a certain timeframe for preparation — a few days, a few weeks, even a few months, depending on the scope of your project.

And then create a schedule within that schedule. What time will you do your research each day? First thing in the morning? In the afternoon, right after you exercise? Whenever it is, make sure you're actually working during that time, not procrastinating.

Spreading out your preparation like this — a little each day — is ideal for a couple reasons. First, it takes away the anxiety and stress of having to cram all your research into too little time. It acknowledges that we tend to overestimate what we can accomplish in one day and underestimate what we can accomplish in a week, a month, a year. (Thanks to Chris Guillebeau, author of *The Art of Noncomformity*, for that one.)

Second, it gives the intuitive, connection-making part of your brain time to process what you've learned. Sort of like how spaghetti sauce tastes better the next day. The ingredients have had time to meld and mingle. You'll start to become aware of where you need more information and where you don't need so much.

RESEARCHING IN STAGES

Think of your research as unfolding in two stages, preliminary and in-depth.

Preliminary research is the fun part. It's one of the few times in life where surfing the Internet can be considered "productive work." So take advantage of that, right? Especially since you've been careful to pick potential concepts that interest you.

In-depth research is where you start exploring the question or questions you're asking. As you're poking around, ask yourself if your question is "thick" enough to sustain your paper. Is there enough information out there for you to write a piece of the scope and length required?

Also in this stage, be honest with yourself about your own interest level. Maybe your concept sounded fun when you first thought of it, but it turns out to be... meh.

If your topic isn't thick enough, or it bores you, ditch it. No tears, no sentimentality. Try it. Throwing stuff away is liberating! One caveat: If you notice yourself ditching stuff all the time, the balance may be tipping toward procrastination or self-defeat. You're looking for an engaging topic, not the perfect one.

If your topic passes both tests, you can move on to primary research. This is where you dive deeper. You print out the sources you found online and read them thoroughly. You go to the library, check out books. You read and absorb and take notes and think.

CREATING YOUR ROAD MAP

When your research period has ended, make a road map. Important: This can be a traditional outline if you want, but a lot of us are afraid of outlines because Mrs. Dorian from sixth grade made us do them and they were really boring and rigid and a ton of work. So your road map does not have to be an outline! There are no Roman numerals required, no lower-case letters or bullet points indented just so.

A road map is simpler. It's a list of points you want to cover. Nothing more, nothing less. Write in full sentences if you want. Write in phrases. Write in Ancient Greek. Use crayons. Number them or not. Doesn't matter. Just get them out in front of you.

Purge! Spew! Now is not the time to be neat and precise. Then, after all the points have emerged from your brain, arrange them in an order that makes some sense to you.

Making a road map does not need to be a days-long or even hours-long process. You don't even have to refer to your research notes much. What sticks in your head most? That's probably the important stuff.

The road map lets you see the big picture of your piece. Instead of stepping into the dark woods of writing with no trail markers or guide, you've got a route.

If you typed your road map, print it out. Then tack it to your wall or keep it on your desk. It will be visible to you when you're writing, a reassuring reminder of where to go next. A talisman for dealing with the fears of "I don't know what I'm doing next!" and "I'm not good enough!"

Just like a real road map on a road trip, or your GPS system, you don't have to follow yours slavishly once you start. You'll find better routes as you go, or discover something you've missed. When that happens, give yourself permission to change course.

The idea is to take that first step from preparation to writing. To move from what others have said to what you are going to say. It's a lot less intimidating than jumping in at the deep end.

MAINTAIN FORWARD MOMENTUM
AKA Let your first draft be messy (and maybe fun)

Once you've got your road map and you're ready to write, you can do just that: Write. Don't edit or revise yet, just write.

We're so tempted when we write to look backward. Doing this feels comfortable because it keeps us from having to push ahead into uncharted territory.

Oh! we think. That sentence I just wrote would be so much better if I changed the first word to "when" rather than "while"! Or maybe that quotation doesn't need to be quite so long….

An hour later, you've still got three sentences out of the 30 pages you need.

It's not that your revision ideas are bad. Both the examples above may well improve your paper. Still, resist the temptation to edit yourself as you go. As Michael Hyatt says in his book *Platform*, writing and editing at the same time requires you to switch back and forth constantly between the two sides of your brain (the right, intuitive side for the writing; the left, logical side for editing). You'll have plenty of time to edit your work later (see p. 31).

Revising as you go can drag you into the quicksand of perfectionism and procrastination. It empowers the inner critic, the voice that's constantly telling you what a bad writer you are. Worse, it takes away any sense of exploration, which is your best hope of having any fun at all while you write your first draft. (And yes! If you give up being perfect, writing a first draft can be fun.)

As you're writing, you'll often get a good idea for an earlier section. Try to note this on a piece of paper or in a separate file and keep moving on. Then go back later and make the change.

When you're writing your first draft, imagine that you're a dog who's just had surgery. You're wearing one of those plastic cones around your head that prevent you from turning to gnaw at the scar on your back. Worry about the scars later, and for now get on with the business of frolicking and sniffing out squirrels.

TAKE YOUR DRAFT ON A DATE
AKA *How to stop fearing revision*

When you're done with your first draft, your impulse may be to squeeze your eyes shut, pinch your nose, and turn it in. "Phew. Done with *that* piece of twaddle."

Don't treat your creation like that! Instead, take it on a date. (Credit for the date idea goes to the novelist and essayist Ann Hood, who recommends this process for honing manuscripts.)

First, though, print it out. Computers are no fun on dates, and you've spent plenty of time staring zombie-like at your screen anyway.

Get your printed copy and a pen, and take your pages to a coffee shop or a park or even a bar if you think you can concentrate there. Somewhere enjoyable, but where you're unlikely to run into a million people you know. This is about you and your work — you don't want any third or fourth wheels to disturb you.

And then read the whole thing through in one sitting (or if it's really long, as much as you can). This isn't about correcting mechanical errors like spelling and grammar, or even strengthening your sentences. You can do those things, of course, but your focus should be on content. Look at the big picture. Are you getting your points across in a persuasive way? Was there something you missed? Something you could take out? Take what Hillary Rettig (*The Seven Secrets of the Prolific*) calls a "fast, light" approach to correcting these bigger problems. Do your best to make them better and then move on. Don't brood or stop. Keep going. You can always take another pass later.

Open your heart to your date. Write all over it. The two of you aren't strangers, so you can really be honest. "You know, paper, I just don't think this paragraph is working..." Write some new ideas, even whole sentences or paragraphs, to replace the old.

THEN go back to your computer and make changes. Do the fussy stuff like checking spelling and grammar. And from your date is born... a second draft! Things went well between you two, apparently. Ideally, you'll have time to go out again and get even better acquainted.

There is such a thing as over-revising, but that usually only starts to happen after multiple revisions and many weeks — an amount of time you're unlikely to face in an academic or professional setting.

We're all on tight timeframes, but if you can wait a day or two (or even longer) between finishing your draft and going on your date, that's ideal. The extra distance will let you view your ideas with a more objective perspective — almost like an outside reader would.

How much time to allow for revision? It depends on the paper and your style of working. Just try to allow enough space for both distance and revision. If you can squeeze in a couple rounds of this, all the better.

ASK FOR FEEDBACK

One of the most helpful things you can do to improve your writing is to ask people read it and give you feedback.

You have to do this with care, though.

First, ask more than one person. If you ask only one, you'll be tempted to take everything they say as gospel. With two or more, you can look for consensus. Is more than one person making the same point about your piece? If so, you should probably address that concern. If not, and you disagree with the point, it's something you can disregard.

Second, coach people in giving you feedback that will be useful to you. Ask them specific questions. For example: Does this section come across as too preachy? Am I arguing a specific point effectively? Also, ask them to tell you what they think is *working* in the piece, not just what isn't. You're only human, and you need encouragement to go along with the criticism.

LETTING GO
AKA Your revision(s) won't be perfect, either

There's no such thing as perfection. We all know that intellectually, but for many of us there's a nagging emotional voice that says something like this: "But if I'm not perfect, I won't be loved! I may even be reviled!" The voice comes up very commonly in writing, because writing, like all creative activities, is an act of self-revelation (to varying degrees depending on the project).

If you hear that voice, it can help to think about where it's coming from. Did you receive harsh feedback from a teacher or family member who instilled that ideal of perfection in you? Were you always an overachiever who learned that striving for perfection was the way to win approval from others?

Brene Brown (*The Gifts of Imperfection*) says this about perfectionism:

> "Perfectionism is self-destructive simply because there's no such thing as perfect. Perfection is an unattainable goal."

By trying to be perfect, we set ourselves up to remain stuck.

Perfectionism becomes a particular pitfall in the revision process, which by definition is about honing and improving your first (maybe messy) draft. So how do you know when to stop revising and let something go?

Again, there's no hard and fast rule. (In fact, the idea that there is a hard and fast rule smacks of perfectionism.) You have to develop an internal gauge about what's good enough — just as in every other aspect of your life. And remember that you won't always feel 100 percent, absolutely, positively fantastic about everything you put out into the world.

There's no such thing as perfection, but there is such a thing as making your best effort. That's what you're looking to get a sense of: Your best. The point where you can say, "I've done the best I can given the resources, time and knowledge I have at this particular time in my life."

Then you let go and experience the relief of circulating your ideas rather than hoarding them.

USE, DON'T ANTAGONIZE, DEADLINES

We've all been there: Hunched over a computer at 3 a.m in the morning, miserably hacking out a paper that's due at 9 a.m. Most likely, we've underprepared and are scrounging for even halfway decent things to say. We hate the paper, we feel bad about ourselves, we resent our professor or boss for having assigned the thing in the first place. In other words, our world has become a pretty narrow, unenjoyable place.

If you tend to be a deadline-antagonizer, it can be productive (if also scary) to ask why. What's really going on? Possibly you have deep-rooted fears of success or failure that you should discuss with a therapist. Maybe this class or this college or this job is not for you. Tough considerations, but answering them honestly will be a whole lot more productive in the long run than suffering through all-nighters and the resulting mediocre grades or performance reviews.

Sometimes we fool ourselves by saying "But that's how I work best! Under intense pressure!" Bad news: That's giving in to the myth of the creative process as misery. Almost no one does their best work while exhausted, overcaffeinated and hating the world. Sure, once in a while you might get lucky and churn out something decent in this state. But most of the time, the old adage holds true: If you're miserable in the writing, your reader will be miserable in the reading.

Deadlines need respect. They can be super helpful, but only when you use them instead of antagonizing them. Think about it: You yourself don't like to be antagonized, do you? Well, neither do your deadlines.

Using a deadline means you:
Create a realistic work plan for completing your project by that deadline, including time for drafting and revision.

Antagonizing a deadline means you:
Procrastinate until the last minute, when you move into panic mode to get the paper done.

Antagonizing deadlines is a self-defeating tendency. Not only does antagonizing often not give you enough time for the drafting phase, it almost never gives you any time for revision. And as we've seen, much of the real work of writing will happen in revision.

A healthier way to use deadlines is to create a work plan or schedule for yourself. Figure out the deadline and work backwards from there. It's almost like doing math, except easier because there aren't as many numbers. Have a dialogue with yourself or even journal about it. Remember to leave some time for revision.

You'll figure out the balance of research, writing and revision that works best for you as a person and for your individual project as you get more experienced. The key is to come up with a reasonable (not panic-based) plan for how to get there.

Now if there's a voice in your head right now saying: "This is all so left-brained and logical and boring. I'm better off just winging it" — remember that being orderly about your work is actually a way to be more creative. That's because being orderly channels the energy you'd otherwise spend on worrying and procrastination into the writing itself.

REWARD YOURSELF FOR COMPLETING SUB-TASKS

It's tempting, in our workaholic culture, to move directly from a completed task into the next one, with no break or acknowledgment of what we've accomplished. That's a foolproof recipe for stress and misery.

Many artists find it helpful and fun to reward themselves for completing the sub-tasks they complete. The reward could be some type of food you love (this isn't a diet book, kids!), a few minutes on Facebook, even a little happy dance. You wrote your road map? Reward. Wrote a page of your first draft? Reward. Made it through your first revision? Reward.

Rewards reinforce an internal feeling of accomplishment — a sense of joy that's self-generated — rather than an external one. Why wait for someone else to give you permission to be happy, to tell you that you did good work?

HOW TO STOP
HIDING IN YO

UR LANGUAGE

HOW TO STOP HIDING IN YOUR LANGUAGE

This next section is about language. It's best to avoid thinking about this section too much while you're in the research or drafting stage, because thinking too much about language while you're in those stages will only slow you down. And you don't want to slow down while you're researching and writing. You want to find your groove and let yourself be messy.

So if you're trying to crank out some research and a first draft, put this book down now and come back when you're done.

HOW WE HIDE IN LANGUAGE

Language is a writer's last hiding place. After we've overcome the fear of actually producing work in the first place using the methods above, there are still nooks and crannies in the words themselves where we can obscure ourselves and our true meaning.

The good news is that language is the easiest component of insecure writing to fix. If you've done poor research, or didn't ask yourself enough questions about your paper, or skipped making a road map — those are far harder problems to fix later. If writing were a house, process would be the foundation, whereas language would be the finishes and siding.

Sure, language matters. It's important. But it's always, always secondary to the structure or substance of your work. You will never be able to make poor content good by making it pretty or polished. That's the Gorgiastic prose my professor warned me about long ago (see p. 10).

So again, worry about this stuff only once you're in the revision phase. Eventually, a lot of these tips will become second-nature.

WHAT DOES 'HIDING IN THE LANGUAGE' MEAN?

Chances are, some teacher in your past has scrawled "passive voice" or "comma splice" in red pen in the margin of one of your papers. Maybe with a frowny face alongside it. And you said, "Yeah? So what?"

Your question was a good one. What's the point of all these rules? If people understand what you're writing, isn't that good enough?

Again, we come back to the idea of hiding. The best language guidelines aren't just nit-picky rules crafted by anal-retentive teachers. Instead, the best language rules keep you from hiding. They force you out into the open, where you have to (dun-dun-DUN) say what you really mean.

When we are disengaged from our writing, language hobgoblins emerge. Clichés. Passive voice. Meandering sentences. Profuse use of "it." If you see a lot of those cropping up, you're shrouding yourself in extra or unclear words because you:

- *Don't know what you want to say*
- *Are afraid to say it*
- *Are disinterested in your topic*
- *Think your content or writing is weak and you need to distract readers with wordiness.*

You can set yourself up to avoid these problems with the process techniques in the previous section. The hobgoblins tend to be scared away by strong early work in those areas.

Then, as you revise, you can use the guidelines below to stay engaged and to say what you mean. Remember, the idea of these guidelines is not to constrain your voice but to reveal it. To keep you clear and open.

You don't have to scrub your writing clean of all the hobgoblins, all the time. Heck, you'll find examples of all of them in this book. Just be aware of them, and use them sparingly. Doing so will keep your language clear and direct.

PREFER ACTIVE VOICE TO PASSIVE VOICE

Passive voice is the vampire of writing. It sucks the blood out of perfectly healthy papers, robbing them of clarity and spirit.

Examples of passive voice:

"It **has not been disclosed** how the transition will be implemented."

"This method **is being recommended** to nearby neighborhoods."

"More than 50 letters of intent **have been signed,** but **it is unknown** how many leases will be secured."

Now look at the same sentences in active voice:

"The County has not disclosed how it will implement the transition."

"Policy makers and citizens' advocates recommended this approach to nearby neighborhoods."

"More than 50 tech companies have signed letters of intent, but the building manager doesn't know how many will commit to a full lease."

In the active voice examples, we're in the real world. We know who's performing the actions. The County, in the first example. Policy makers and advocates, in the second. Tech companies, in the third.

In the passive voice examples, we're in la-la-land, a sort of fifth dimension where Unknown Beings are doing the non-disclosing and recommending and signing of leases.

Like ornate sentences, passive voice tempts us because it has a veneer of formality. Also, it allows us to cop out — to be vague and evasive about who's doing what. Writing in passive voice is easier.

But active voice offers much more substantial rewards. Active voice gives writing specificity and authority. It better engages readers and gives them more information.

To write in active voice, you will need to be clear about who are the actors in your sentences.

Actors hang out in theaters, right? Yes — but you also want them in your sentences. Actors are the people, places or things who DO the actions you're writing about.

Look at this passive-voice sentence:

"Laws were passed that removed previous roadblocks to success."

We don't know who passed those laws. But we do in this active-voice rewrite:

"City Council passed laws that removed previous roadblocks to success."

The sentence becomes both more informative (City Council passed the laws) and more vivid.

The vividness comes from being able to picture a scene (City Council passing a law), rather than just understanding the idea of laws being passed. Readers are visual. So even though this scene may not be Hollywood blockbuster material, it still gives readers something they can picture rather than just understand in the abstract.

Sometimes, the actors are hiding right in our own passive-voice sentences. The word "by" is often a clue. For example, you can switch "The Convention Center was booked by more than 30 organizations…" to the tighter "More than 30 organizations booked the Convention Center."

'TO BE' IS NOT THE ONLY VERB

The English language contains thousands of verbs, and "to be" is just one.

Of course, we need "to be." It's so fundamental, so common, that when we're writing sentences, forms of "to be" (is, was, were, has been, will be, etc.) often come first to mind. So we go ahead and use them.

But an overabundance of "be" verbs signals that you've checked out of your project, and your writing goes limp. Again, readers are visual, and want to picture what's going on. "Be" doesn't give them much of an image. If something simply "is," we picture it sitting there, like a couch potato. Who wants to read about couch potatoes?

Don't get me wrong: You'll still use forms of "to be" a lot. But if you start to notice them cropping up in most of your sentences, see if you can reach into the ocean of other verbs.

'To be' sentences and possible rewrites:

Original: *The most important factor influencing subjects' answers was their mood while taking the questionnaire.*

Rewrite: *Subjects' moods influenced their answers more than any other factor.*

Original: *Hands are a recurring image in the novel.*

Rewrite: *The author describes the movement of characters' hands in nearly every chapter of the novel.*

Like using active voice, using verbs other than "to be" prods you to provide more information, more vividly. That's the opposite of hiding.

Awareness of "to be" also helps with awareness of passive voice, because passive voice needs "to be" to survive. ("Was made," "is written," "has been given," etc.)

Again, you don't have to banish "to be" from your work. But reaching for more active verbs often opens the door to more vivid, more informative writing.

ADDITIONALLY...
AKA Adverbs aren't your friends

They're so lovely, aren't they? Those long words ending in -ly. Additionally. Practically. Virtually. They're like little flowers we can insert in our sentences, giving them extra decoration and oomph....

Wrong. Nine times out of ten, adverbs slow the reader down without adding any real meaning to a sentence. They're the empty calories of writing. In college papers, readers know you're using them to pad your word count.

A quick review: Adverbs modify verbs. They describe the manner in which something is done.

Doesn't sound so bad, right? But like passive voice and long sentences (see next section), people often use adverbs to dress up their writing, to make it sound more formal or intelligent.

Adverbs are often short-cuts that dance around the real facts, or redundancies that reiterate something you say elsewhere. For example: "The mayor destructively imposed a higher sales tax…" Well, what was destructive about it? Either you're not going to explain, in which case the reader will be left to wonder, or the explanation lies somewhere else in the paper, in which case the word is redundant.

The old "less is more" rule comes into play here, too. Remember that your reader will respect you most, and appreciate the time you've saved them, if you say what you mean in as few words as possible.

As with most of these language rules, don't worry too much about adverbs while you're in the drafting stage. But look for them when you're revising. (They're easy to spot: Just look for words ending in -ly, as well as "very," "often" and "just.") Try taking them out, and be honest about whether you've lost any real meaning. At first, doing so may make you feel naked, exposed. That your writing is "too simple." But remember those are all good signs you're no longer hiding.

WRITE SHORTER SENTENCES

Look at the sentences below. Which are you more likely to be engaged by, and to remember?

Most scientists predict the next Ice Age will arrive within 4,000 years.

With respect to the arrival of the next Ice Age, there is widespread debate among researchers in the scientific community about timing; it is asserted by the majority that the next cooling will begin in approximately 4,000 years, but by others that it will begin in as few as 2,000 years or as many as 10,000 years.

LIKE PASSIVE VOICE AND LONG SENTENCES, PEOPLE OFTEN USE ADVERBS TO DRESS UP THEIR WRITING, TO MAKE IT SOUND MORE FORMAL OR INTELLIGENT.

Both sentences give the same amount of real information. But the first sentence makes its point in 75 percent fewer words than the second. Thanks, first sentence! You saved me time and effort.

The second sentence, meanwhile, is a thick swamp of adjectives, passive voice and dependent clauses. In fact, your eyes may have instinctively resisted reading it because they could tell at a glance that doing so would be a slog.

You might also get the sense that the second writer is trying to impress you. Are you impressed? Or do you end up resenting her because she stuffed you so full of unnecessary words?

Not all long sentences are simply wordy for wordy's sake. They do contain a lot of information.

Still, short sentences pack a bigger punch than long ones. They're easier to digest and they have an air of authority about them. Your readers will adore you for using them.

Whenever you see a compound sentence with a conjunction such as "and" or "but" or "however" stringing together two separate parts, consider replacing the conjunction with a period. The separated sentences will be more readable and forceful than the compound version.

The best rule of thumb? Use as few words as possible to say what you need to say. Your readers want information, please, not to gorge themselves on vocabulary.

COMMA SPLICES AND RUN-ON SENTENCES

If passive voice is the vampire of writing, then sentences with comma splices, run-on sentences and semicolons are the Frankenstein's monsters. They're reanimated beasts, strung together of separate parts that should remain independent.

These types of sentences sometimes result from careless grammar. But sometimes they're a type of hiding. That's because — like most types of long sentences — they are aiming to either dazzle readers or to obscure a lack of solid content.

A comma splice happens when you separate two full sentences with a comma instead of a period. Examples:

Ramses asserts that this conclusion does not stand up to scientific examination, it is based on flawed methodology.

Not all long books are boring, they can be entertaining.

In both cases, we've got two complete sentences masquerading as one, with a comma splicing them together Frankenstein-style.

A run-on sentence operates the same way, but doesn't even have a comma, poor thing. For example:

The subject had to depart it was five o'clock.

The fix for both of these situations? Replace the comma (or the complete lack of punctuation) with a period, so that each independent sentence can stand on its own.

Ramses asserts that this conclusion does not stand up to scientific examination. It is based on flawed methodology.

Not all long books are boring. They can be entertaining.

The subject had to depart. It was five o'clock.

A quick note on semicolons (;). They aren't grammatically incorrect, but they do the same work as comma splices and run-ons in that they tie together independent sentences that would often be clearer and more readable on their own. You don't have to avoid them altogether, but when you encounter them in revising, ask yourself if the two sentences they link would be clearer on their own.

THE BEST RULE OF THUMB? USE AS FEW WORDS AS POSSIBLE TO SAY WHAT YOU NEED TO SAY. YOUR READERS WANT INFORMATION, PLEASE, NOT TO GORGE THEMSELVES ON VOCABULARY.

THE "IT" MONSTER

It is tiny. It is unassuming.

But it creeps into your writing like a virus, spreading when you're not paying attention.

What am I talking about? The word "it," of course.

"It" creates vagueness and lack of clarity (types of hiding!) in your work. And that's a problem because lack of clarity sends readers minds' wandering.

In neither of these examples are we quite sure what "it" is:

It is not known how subjects would have responded if researchers had reworded the first question.

(Or any similar construction with "it" at the beginning of a sentence: It is exciting, it is awful, it is my hope…)

Never transport an item to or from an area regardless of how safe it may seem.

The first sentence isn't grammatically incorrect. In fact, people use "it" at the beginning of sentences all the time. But the sentence would be clearer and more efficient if we said instead: "Subjects in the experiment may have responded differently if researchers had reworded the first question." That also takes care of the passive voice in "it is not known."

In the second sentence, "it" could refer to any one of three things that came earlier in the sentence: the item, the area or the act of transporting. ("Transport" instead of "move" is also an example of Fancy Language. See p. 51)

Remember: We want the reader to spend his energy understanding our ideas, not our sentence construction. The writer could say instead "Never transport that item to or from an area regardless of how safe doing so may seem." The phrase "doing so" clarifies that the writer is talking about the act of transporting.

Of course, there are clear uses of "it." For example: "The convention center didn't stop construction until 2014 because the county built it in phases." There, "it" can only refer to "convention center." The meaning is obvious.

When you're revising your paper, let an alarm go off anytime you see "it." The alarm is an apt image, because we write "it" more when we're sleepwalking through a piece.

When the "it" alarm sounds, ask yourself: Is there a way to be clearer or more specific about what I mean here? If so, rewrite.

CLICHÉS: WHO NEEDS 'EM?

I once had the opportunity to interview The Shins, one of my favorite bands. I've never forgotten something the lead singer, James Mercer, told me about the way he writes his lyrics. "Mostly," he said, "I just try to avoid clichés." That practice alone, he said, was enough to push him to say something fresh and honest.

Clichés are phrases that you've heard a million times before. Often, they employ some type of metaphor, so they're tempting to use in writing that has a personal aspect: Essays, fiction, poetry. For example:

His heart raced.

She ran like the wind.

The crime rate spiraled out of control.

But nonfiction and business writing are not immune. "Low-hanging fruit." "Moving forward." Oh, and one of the most overused clichés ever: "Thinking outside the box."

As you revise, look out for phrases like these — ones you've heard so many times before they've become meaningless. See if you can think of another way to say what you mean. Often, you can cut out the offending phrases with little or no impact on your meaning.

FANCY LANGUAGE

Where else but in academic and professional papers do people "utilize" something rather than "use" it? Where else do we say "additionally" instead of "also"? How about "individuals" instead of "people"?

These words try to impress readers by being fancy, but they just slow us down. We understand right away that the writer is trying to be flashy. And why would a writer be flashy with her language if she were confident in the basic value of her points?

We're almost always better off when we ~~utilize~~ use everyday vocabulary rather than dazzlers. Just write what you mean, and let the language support that in the least intrusive way possible.

IN CL

OSING

So you've got all
that, right?

And you'll be able
to write without hiding
forevermore?

Just kidding. Think of reading this, or any other writing advice book, as one more step toward freer writing. Sometimes, or maybe often, you'll forget these guidelines and find yourself stuck. No big deal. Usually, the answer is to take a deep breath, maybe a short break — and then start writing again. And to remind yourself that the draft you're working on now, whether it's the first or the fourth, doesn't need to be perfect.

The great thing is that as you keep writing, you'll become more aware of the ways you hide. Maybe you're a deadline pusher. Maybe you have trouble allowing yourself to pick topics that interest *you*. Maybe you stick to a writing routine that no longer works for you. Or you over-research. As you gain self-knowledge, you'll be able to check your habits and push yourself to move past them.

I struggle most with the idea of not looking back. I love to look back and tweak and rework as I go. But I'm aware of that tendency, and over time I've gotten better at catching myself — or at least limiting the time I spend revising as I go.

Keep in mind that even when you write something that feels very "unhidden" to you, you may not get universal acclaim from every single person in the world. Some coworker or professor or anonymous commenter on the Internet (they're the meanest) may call your work garbage. That's no fun, but this is just one piece of writing and theirs is just one opinion. Take the long view that learning to write without hiding is a lifelong process.

The most important thing is to get started. Let yourself wobble and make mistakes on your way to being heard.

FURTHER READING

Brown, Brene. *The Gifts of Imperfection: Let Go of Who You Think You're Supposed to Be and Embrace Who You Are.* Hazelden, 2010.

Fried, Jason. *Rework.* Random House, 2010.

Godin, Seth. *The Icarus Deception: How High Will You Fly?* Penguin, 2012.

Guillebeau, Chris. *The Art of Nonconformity: Set Your Own Rules, Live the Life You Want and Change the World.* Penguin, 2010.

Hyatt, Michael. *Platform: Get Noticed in Noisy World.* Thomas Nelson, 2012.

King, Stephen. *On Writing: A Memoir of the Craft.* Scribner, 2000.

Kleon, Austin. *Steal Like an Artist: 10 Things No One Told You About Being Creative.* Workman Publishing Co., 2012.

Lamott, Anne. *Bird by Bird: Some Instructions on Writing and Life.* Random House, 1994.

Rettig, Hillary. *The 7 Secrets of the Prolific: The Definitive Guide to Overcoming Procrastination, Perfectionism, and Writer's Block.* Infinite Art, 2011.

Who made this?

BEAGLE

Beagle is the creative collaboration of Justin Glanville [writer], Julia Kuo [illustrator] and Lee Zelenak [designer]. We're like a band, except we make books instead of music. We enjoy demystifying complex topics and discovering the unfamiliar in the familiar — all while having fun and thinking deep thoughts. *Writing Without Hiding* is our second book. Our first was *New to Cleveland: A Guide to (Re)Discovering the City*. Our next will be about exploring Easter Island.

We'd love to hear from you. You can visit us online at www.the-beagle.com

Justin Glanville is a freelance writer. He is a former reporter for The Associated Press and has taught college-level courses on professional writing. He is working on a novel and a supernatural podcast series. Find him at www.justinglanville.com

Julia Kuo is a freelance illustrator working out of Chicago. Her clients include Simon & Schuster, Little Brown & Co., Universal Music Group, Capitol Records, American Greetings, and the New York Times. You can find her work online at www.juliakuo.com.

Lee Zelenak is a graphic designer and educator. Formerly, he was a Senior Designer for President Barack Obama's 2012 re-election campaign. Currently, he is the Creative Director and Managing Partner of Kiddo Design Collect. You can find them at www.kiddo-design.com

Heartfelt thanks to: Seth Beattie, Christine Borne, Megan Jones, Daniel McDonald and Deanna Palermo

www.ingramcontent.com/pod-product-compliance
Lightning Source LLC
Chambersburg PA
CBHW041528090426
42736CB00036B/233